V

C000177736

Directiona̶l̶ ̶̶i̶̶n̶̶f̶̶l̶̶u̶̶e̶̶n̶̶c̶̶e̶̶s̶ ̶o̶n̶
Human Affairs

*A guidebook for effective living within the
structures and spaces of our modern society.*

Bangalore Niranjan Babu

Foreword by A.R. Natarajan & Dr. Sarada Natarajan

LOTUS
PRESS

Volume 2

First US Edition, 2021

ISBN: 978-1-6086-9266-8

Library of Congress Control Number: 2020948539

Published by:
Lotus Press,
P.O. Box 325, Twin Lakes, Wisconsin 53181 USA
www.lotuspress.com
lotuspress@lotuspress.com
800-824-6396

This book is respectfully dedicated
to my revered parents
Dr. B.V. Raman and Smt Rajeswari Raman
for making me what I am today.

MOTHER'S BLESSINGS
(Received in 2006)

I am happy to say a few words about my son Niranjan Babu and his book **Vastu – Diectional Influences on Human Affairs**.

His books have received much acclaim from the discerning readers of India and abroad.

In this book, Niranjan Babu goes deeper into the fascinating subject of Vastu and its influences on Human Affairs as varied as Old Age Homes and Corporate Structures. Niranjan Babu has made a mark for himself on the Vastu scene and has lectured, conducted workshops and given consultations in India and oversears.

I bless him from my heart and wish him all success in his endeavor to properly educate the reader on the importance of this ancient science which is a *Upaveda* and rightly called *Sthapathya Veda*.

Rajeswari Raman
Director, Sri Surya Prakash Institute of
Yoga for Women, Bangalore.
Chairperson, Raman & Rajeswari Research
Foundation, Regd.

Vastu Sastra, abbreviated as Vastu, is one of the ancient scriptures of India. It deals with the science of Indian architecture. It is intended to take the advantages of Cosmo Terrestrial Energies in all buildings. Its embrace therefore covers Temples, Residential Apartments, Homes for the Senior Citizens, Interiors of any working place.

The author of the book Mr. Niranjan Babu, is an expert in Vastu. He is a reputed author of many books in this field. In this book, he emphasizes Vastu's Directional Influences on Human Affairs. He has given me extracts from this book. His expertise is evident throughout, for he places himself in the shoes of those who are using different walks of life. The core purpose of this book is to give each and every one a working knowledge about this vast scripture the use of which is a must for everyone who desires happiness in his home or harmony in the working environment.

I am sure that this book will sell well like his earlier books on the subject.

I would like to thank Mr. Niranjan Babu, for giving me this opportunity of writing the 'Foreword' for this valuable book. We have common bonds through our love and devotion to Bhagavan Sri Ramana Maharshi. His faith in Sri Ramana has redoubled after the miraculous way his life was saved in a motor accident. About three years ago, I would say, Ramana made me think of him and the need for using his expertise in Vastu for the Ramana Maharshi Heritage Building. Discussions with him, made it abundantly clear to us that every rule of Vastu had been transgressed to a greater or lesser extent because of our idea that since we are not having any personal profit motive, we could treat this as a 'Devalaya' and not a 'Manushalaya'. He explained why even though, there is no profit making motive, the activities are for generating profit for ploughing back the service to Bhagavan Ramana. Therefore it should be treated as 'Manushalaya'. Only the Meditation Hall could be called 'Devalaya'. On the basis of his advice, which we accepted, he created several 'upamandalas' to solve the problem and this has definitely changed the scenario. Our faith in Vastu itself has become so strong that in the building which we are constructing in honor of Bhagavan Sri Ramana Maharshi, on the occasion of his 125th

Birth Year, the entire planning of the building has been entrusted to him and the architect is to work in co-ordination with him to ensure that the modern and ancient scriptures are taken advantage of.

At the shrine of Bhagavan Sri Ramana Maharshi, in Bangalore, he has also made many valuable suggestions, including the need for a continuous flow of water.

Apart from his own deep knowledge of the subject, his strength is also in the fact that he has a total faith in the scriptural statement 'Matru Devobhava' and 'Pitru Devobhava' and regards Mother and Father as embodiments of God. He never omits to refer to his father Dr. B.V Raman, who restored people's faith in over fifty years. His mother Smt. Rajeswari Raman, is a master of Yoga Sastra and is using this knowledge fo the benefit of a large number of women, who have the fortune to be her students.

Another strength of Niranjan Babu is the way he explains to the clients and friends the different aspects of Vastu so that they too can partake of the knowledge. He works very hard to ensure that his knowledge is utilized to the maximum extent possible.

It is my strong wish and desire that Bhagavan Ramana may give him long life and same mental alertness to serve the community for many years to come.

A.R. Natarajan
President
Ramana Maharshi Centre for Learning

(We are immensely pleased that Dr. Sarada Natarajan, President of Ramana Maharishi Centre of Learning, Bangalore and the daughter of Sri A. R. Natarajan has kindly given the Foreward to the present edition being brought out by Lotus Press, Twin Lakes, Wisconsin. We are thankful to her for accepting our request to to give the foreword for this edition.)

FOREWORD FOR THE USA EDITION BY DR. SARADA NATARAJAN

It was my privilege to meet Sri Niranjan Babu along with my father in 2001 when we opened the **Ramana Maharshi Heritage Auditorium** and the office block. What struck me then was the gentle manner in which he gave his guidance according to the principles of Vastu Sastra. He understood the situation in which we were placed, that we had sought his guidance after the building was constructed and gave guidelines that was possible for us to execute. He made us feel a part of the entire process of inviting the positive energies to our space.

I also found that while his suggestions had an impact that was subtle, they also had a practical import at a simple level. For instance, the light and air may be felt to the best advantage in the position that he suggested for our seating. This is of great relevance in the context of the present book that details the Influence of Vastu on Human Affairs. Surely an understanding of Vastu at a basic level through the insights shared in this book would enable people to take better decisions regarding the use of spaces in every context.

In my first meeting with Sri Niranjan Babu one instance remains etched in my mind. When he came to my father's office space he asked him 'Who is the boss here?' My father replied immediately, 'Bhagavan Sri Ramana Maharshi'. Niranjan Babu gave his sweet smile. 'In the south west corner of the room, on a pedestal that is heavy, place the picture of Bhagavan Ramana', he said. That picture still presides over the room and the entire Centre. Later on my father consulted him before commencing construction of the new archival block and it was designed in accordance with the principles of Vastu Shastra.

I recently had the joy of inviting him for guiding us about the renovation of the **Ramana Maharshi Auditorium**. He came with his customary kindness and devotion to Bhagavan Ramana. Never any sense of hurry –

as Ramana says our life should be 'unhurried and recollected'. He gave us his invaluable guidance for the project. He also accepted to be our advisor for all projects of the Centre. We thank him for doing so. I have felt that his advice is not only based on his in-depth knowledge of the subject but is also springing from an intuitive approach to it based on his devotion.

I join my father's prayer to Bhagavan Ramana to give him life and strength to continue his service to society through his knowledge and insight into Vastu. I thank him for giving me an opportunity to add to my father's foreword to this extremely valuable publication and in this manner to express our Centre's gratitude to him.

Dr. Sarada Natarajan
President, Ramana Maharshi Centre for Learning
April 24, 2020

PREFACE TO THE FIRST EDITION

It gives me immense happiness to present my esteemed readers, **Vastu - Directional Influences on Human Affairs**.

In 1995, my revered father Dr. B. V. Raman, Founder- Editor of **The Astrological Magazine** conducted the First All India Symposium on Vastu. Eminent scholars from all over India spoke on this science and created awareness. Today, Vastu is gaining global recognition. Buildings are being constructed and/or modified on Vastu principles with good results.

In this book, I have endeavored to highlight the importance of various aspects of Vastu like orientation, topography, soil evaluation, foundations, celestial and terrestrial energies, primary elements of nature and their global application to temples and modern buildings. Some of the topics have appeared in the columns of our **The Astrological Magazine**. I hope that this book of mine will motivate the readers to make use of this ancient science of architecture and help them to live a life of good health, happiness and contentment.

The esteemed public received my earlier books well and I am sure the readers will find this book not only interesting but practically applicable to various aspects of construction. I hope that this book will also be received by my esteemed readers with the same enthusiasm. One of the chapters talks about the power of the pyramids (or shikaras) interfacing ancient wisdom with modern construction.

My study and research in Vastu have been absolutely due to the encouragement and guidance of my revered parents, Dr. B. V. Raman and Mrs. Rajeswari Raman (Director. Sri Surva Prakash Institute of Yoga for Women, Bangalore, India.)

I thank Mr. A. R. Natarajan for his valuable foreword. I thank Dr. Bangalore Sureshwara of Chicago for his scholarly introduction and Mr. William Levacy of Los Angeles for his illuminating observations on the contents of my book.

I acknowledge my wife's (Umarani Niranjan Babu) and my children's (Raman Suprajarama and Raman Siddhartha) encouragement, assistance and enthusiastic support and providing me the necessary impetus and energy needed in my writings over the years.

I thank Dr. Sarada Natarajan for her secondary foreword.

I also express my thanks to Lotus Press for publishing this American edition of the book. My warm regards to Mr. Santosh Krinsky and his staff.

Bangalore Niranjan Babu

PREFACE TO THE US EDITION

It gives me much happiness that Mr. Santosh Krinsky has kindly accepted to bring this edition of my book **Handbook of Vastu Directional Influences on Human Affairs.** This book has been a best seller and covers many important aspects of Vastu Shastra as varied as Orientation, Topography, Foundations, Soil Evaluation, Senior Citizen Homes, Apartments, Colour Therapy, Dwellings and Security, Cosmo Terrestrial Energies and Natural Calamities.

I thank my wife and my children for the support they have given me in bringing out this edition. Mr. Santosh Krinsky and his staff have been extremely cordial in interacting with me online during this period of the pandemic. I thank them for publishing this book of mine for the benefit of the global community.

Bangalore Niranjan Babu

INTRODUCTORY NOTE

Vastu Shastra or Vastu, as is commonly referred to these days is a part of the Vedas, the knowledge bequeathed to us over thousands of years ago by the sages and seers, whose learning and wisdom were immense and immeasurable by any standards available to humanity. These ancient seers and sages constantly emphasized that not only humans must live with nature in a humane way but also more importantly every action of a person or society was to use the various energies provided by nature to benefit the mankind-at-large. The magic words in their lives were affection and magnanimity. Based on their eternal noble thinking and ideas, they have provided us a giant umbrella of knowledge that is also well integrated with wisdom. The vast measurable knowledge that we have bequeathed from the ancient sages and seers are now defined under various areas, such as Dharma Sastras, Vedic Astrology, Vastu Shastra, Ayurveda, etc.

Vastu Sastra is one source of energy that can immensely help us to make our lives balanced and free us from material and mental conflicts. A significant portion of the vast literature that we have inherited from our sages and seers are written in a coded language and often cannot be literally applied to the conditions and situations prevalent in today's world. The coded literature is like the little precious piece of diamond that is hidden in a large piece of rock. An average person will look at the rock and is unable to see that a gem is carefully hidden in the rock. In a similar fashion, most people will look at the coded literature and literally translate them. Therefore, they provide rather limited information that can be applied to design and construction of residential, business, commercial buildings and many others. Understanding the coded language contained within the ancient Vastu treatises requires more than a lifetime of dedicated learning and immeasurable practical experience. One needs a sage or scholar with the knowledge, wisdom and experience to de-codify specific information that is subtle and hidden in various treatises to apply for the location and design of kitchen, pooja room, family room, etc., and the various components contained within each one of them.

Mr. Niranjan Babu needs no introduction, since he has already shown that he is one of the limited number of persons to not only have in-depth knowledge in Vastu Shastra but more importantly has the skill and ability to de-codify the often embedded and challenging information contained in the extraordinary classical texts. And he has synthesized them in such a manner so that the valuable information can be carefully and appropriately applied to the various varieties of modern buildings, rooms, etc. Mr. Niranjan Babu has the intuitive ability to present what normally appears to be complicated information in a classical text into easily understandable language of even a common person. It is no surprise that his books are popular and bestselling books. In this informational book **Handbook of Vastu - Directional Influences on Human Affairs**, he has put in a lot of effort to also include some of his research findings pertaining to orientation and directions. The application of traditional Vastu principles to apartments, relative to orientation and directions, has a lot of limitations. Here, Mr. Niranjan Babu has carefully studied the Vastu principles covering directions and orientations, so that they can be applied to not only to the design of the whole apartment complex but even to the design of a single apartment within the complex, while also considering the financial and other constraints. Verbatim application of certain Vastu principles can become a nightmare for people with limited resources and here we see Mr. Niranjan Babu at his best in presenting only the essential Vastu requirements that also prompt the well being of the individual and society. Modern times have not only created wealth but have also, unfortunately, created great concern and fear regarding safety and security for the people and society-at-large. Vastu guidelines have been provided covering the security aspect for the individual as well as for the dwelling. Other important and contemporary topics like colour therapy, senior citizens and old age homes have been included in this book. This book fills a big void that exists in the current available literature covering practical application of Vastu principles to homes, apartments and other buildings.

The author has to be congratulated for taking a difficult subject with vast information and presenting it in an easy to understand manner while not compromising on the essential required details of Vastu, particularly as related to practical design and construction. This is one reference book that every student and practitioner of Vastu, including architects, construction & structural engineers, builders and building inspectors must have at all times.

Dr. Bangalore Sureshwara, USA

(Dr. Bangalore Sureshwara has been actively involved in the research study of the application of Ramayana, Mahabharatha, Sri Bhagavad Gita, Hindu Theology, and Vedic Astrology in modern life. His lectures, seminars, workshops and writings on the above subjects have been well-received in India and USA.

Dr. Sureshwara studied Vedic Astrolgy under his illustrious father Dr. B.V. Raman. He was the principal speaker on Vedic Astrology at The Second Parliament of the World's Religions held in Chicago in August-September 1993. He has been a distinguished contributor to **The Astrological Magazine**, Asia's leading Vedic Astrology journal. Dr. B.V. Raman was its Editor from 1932 to 1998.

Dr. Sureshwara is the author of the acclaimed book "Ramayana: Values, Then and Now." Professor Sureshwara has taught "Ramayana and Management", "Bhagavad Gita and Management" and related courses/ seminars to MBA students.

Dr. B. Sureshwara has a Bachelor of Engineering from Mysore University (India) and Master's & Doctorate in Engineering from the University of Notre Dame (USA). He has taught Engineering at undergraduate and post-graduate levels. His extensive industry experiences include Civil, Structural, Mechanical and Aerospace Engineering.)

OBSERVATIONS

Vastu, the Science of Vedic architecture, has its roots in the ancient Vedic tradition of India that views ourselves, our bodies, and our environment as components integrated into one unified field of natural law.

Mr. Niranjan Babu, in his new book **Vastu Directional Influences on Human Affairs**, leads us masterfully through the integrated knowledge of Vastu. He explains Vastu principles with a thoroughness and clarity that expresses his deep knowledge and many years of experience. We learn from Niranjan Babu that Vastu influences can be identified through the integrating links of the five elements or 'panchabhutas'. We see the foundations of Vastu captured within the healing arts of Ayuveda, the Vedic science of health. We see how the rhythms of nature identified in Vastu have their counterpart in Vedic music. A building is likened to a musical instrument playing the harmonies of nature.

The ancient guidelines of Vastu are also applied to practical matters of modern living. We are not only given tips on how to identify appropriate residential and business buildings but also how to choose the best of the present apartment buildings we see in modern cities. As we know that people are living longer these days and the care and responsibilities towards our elders is an ever increasing concern. Niranjan Babu's book provides us with guidance in using Vastu to make parents' and grandparents' later years a time of comfort and joy.

The technology of Vastu is also relevant in fortifying modern structures to more ably survive natural disasters. We are told of some protective measures, seen in examples of ancient Mohenjodaro and Harappa of India, that might even make some of us who live in earthquake zones able to sleep a bit better at night. For those who want an integrated view of the wonderful science of Vastu, readers will find **Vastu Directional Influences on Human Affairs** a guidebook for effective living within the structures and spaces of our modern society.

William R. Levacy
Los Angeles, California, USA, 2006

(Dr. William Levacy passed away in February 2018. With a degree in literature, a master's and a doctorate in education with specialization in Human Performance Improvement, he was the author of several best-selling books on Vedic Astrology - *Beneath a Vedic Sky, Beneath a Vedic Sun* and *Vedic Astrology, Simply Put.* He was a regular contributor to **The Astrological Magazine** and a good friend of the Raman family. He developed a computer generated/printed ephemeris used by **The Astrological Magazine**. He was practising the science of Vedic Astrology for more than three decades. He was the recipient of very many awards. Raman & Rajeswari Research Foundation honored him twice with the titles of *Jyothisha Maha Sagara* and *Jyothisha Jnana Sagara*.

Apart from his scholarship in Vedic Astrology, he worked as a management consultant for the Aerospace industry. He trained many people and did many projects related to business process re-engineering, performance measurement, and team building.

Dr. Bill Levacy was a wonderful person, kind and considerate and a man of varied accomplishments. Dr. Bill's demise has left a deep void and has left the entire astrological world in deep grief.)

Table of Contents

1

Introduction

Vastu or Vastu Shastra, the ancient science of Indian architecture, and Jyotisha or Vedic Astrology are integral parts of Vedas, the vast knowledge bequeathed to us by great sages of India. Vastu is both a science and art and aims at making human habitation not only a thing of beauty and joy but more importantly in providing in the long run a level of comfort, delight and happiness to the inhabitants.

The science of Vastu takes into primary consideration the energies radiating from the four directions viz., North, East, South and West. It explains in simple but in an effective manner the selection of site, construction of a residence, apartment, business complex, hospital complex, educational complex, homes for the senior citizens and handicapped, temples, ashrams, etc. as well as the placement of various rooms in these buildings. It also extends to such fields as construction of ports, townships or cities.

Vastu is more than the science of modern architecture. It also encompasses the science of cosmology, astronomy, metaphysics, geography and geology. The cosmological aspect is best illustrated by observing the solar system. In the vast universe, apart from the earth that we live in, there are many other systems, including planetary systems, which influence or impact human lives.

The astronomical aspect is best demonstrated by the Ayadi Shadvarga or six building formulae that are used in defining the various measurements of temples and residences. Varahamihira in his **Brihat Samhita** tells us that he "will now explain for the happiness of the astronomers and astrologers, the science of architecture that has come down from Brahma through a steady line of intellectuals."

The metaphysical aspect is best understood when one becomes aware of the importance of drawing the Vastu Purusha mandala or plan before a building construction is initiated. The *mandala* symbolizes the metaphysical principle of the all-encompassing celestial energies.

Coming to the geographical and geological facets of Vastu Shastra, the ancient texts saw the importance of studying the topography of the land and the surroundings apart from studying the whole universe with its array of stars, planets, continents, rivers, seas, mountains etc. The examination of soil in terms of sound, touch, smell, taste and color highlight the geological aspects of this great science. In a nutshell, under the umbrella of Vastu Shastra, information and knowledge from a variety of subjects are included.

Astrological Indications

The fourth house in a horoscope indicates information covering property and inheritance. The lords of the second, fourth and the twelfth in kendras or trikonas, when well placed, indicate smoothness in matters pertaining to houses and other forms of property. The fourth lord in Lagna or in the seventh indicates acquisition of a house without much difficulty. On the other hand, if the lord of the fourth is in the eighth, afflicted or debilitated, it denotes the possible denial of land and house. Property is also indicated, if Venus is posited in the fourth house.

When Mars occupies the fourth, it indicates that the person can own a house but the house cannot bring happiness to the individual. If the Sun is in the fourth house, inheritance is indicated. If Ketu is in the fourth, then there is the possibility of the person being denied or deprived of property. The results indicated above get modified by aspects and conjunctions of other planets. A collective and careful approach is necessary when evaluating a horoscope.

Selection of Site

Much importance needs to be given to the selection of a site. It is recommended that plots which are not oriented to cardinal directions, viz., North, East, South and West are to be avoided.

Select rectangular or square sites. The length and breadth need to be in a prescribed ratio. While for temples a square site is best, for human habitations a 1:2 site is good.

Sites sloping down towards North and East are good for health, wealth and success in life.

Plots or sites in the shape of a triangle, circle or oval and other irregular shape need to be avoided.

Growth of sites in wrong zones is not advisable. Sital growth in the South- west, Southeast and Northwest are normally not recommended.

People like to go in for corner sites, While corner sites may be appealing, but one needs to be careful in selecting them in that they need to satisfy specific aspects of Vastu.

Orient the building to the cardinal directions viz., North, East, West and South.

Landscaping

Gardening or Landscaping has been connected closely with town planning and house building. Ancient masters have laid down certain guidelines for planting and placement of trees. It is considered that the goddess of wealth symbolically lives for generations in the house in which the *Bilva* (Aegle Marmelos) or *Bael* tree is planted.

Floor Plans

Thirty-two plans for construction are elaborated. These plans are called *Vastu Purusha Mandalas* beginning from the single (1x1) module *mandala* known as the *Sakala* to the 1024 (32x32) modules *mandala* called *Indrakanta*. The *Sakala* is recommended for *homakundas* or fire altars and the *Indrakanta* for planning of towns and cities.

The *Paramasyika Mandala* or the 81 (9x9) modules plan is ideal for residential buildings. The centre nine modules of the mandala relate to the *Brahmasthana* and the central module is called *Brahma Nabhi* or *Brahma*

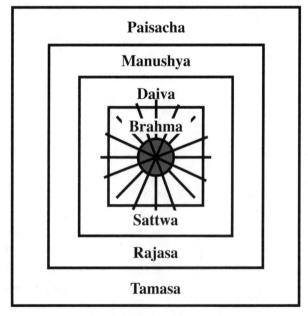

Paisacha

Manushya

Daiva

Brahma

Sattwa

Rajasa

Tamasa

Zones of an Area

Fig. 01.01

Bindu. The *Vastu Purusha Mandala* is divided into four concentric zones. The central zone is called the *Brahmasthana* or the space corresponding to total awareness. The next three zones are *Daiva, Manushya* and *Paisacha* zones and are said to denote enlightenment, consciousness and grossness, respectively. The terms *Daiva, Manushya* and *Paisacha* perhaps denote the energy flow pattern which begins from the center or *brahmabindu* which is the point of awareness and flows outward as three basic *Gunas* viz. *Satwa* (calm), *Rajas* (active), and *Tamas* (inactive.)

A building structure is normally recommended in the *Daiva* and *Manushya* zones. Vastu is particularly concerned with the *panchamahabhootas* and studies the five elements viz., earth, water, fire, wind and cosmic space. Proper selection of a site, placement of water bodies, cooking areas, hearth and ovens, doors and windows and open space within the building and in the plot are said to infuse life energy.

Human Habitations

In residential houses, the verandah (front room or lobby) and the living room can be in any sector based on the orientation but preferred in the North and East. Master bedrooms can be in the South, West and Southwest, rooms for boys can be in the South, Southeast and East, rooms for the girls can be in the North, Northwest and West, rooms for the elders and study rooms for youngsters can be in the Northeast and East.

Newly married couples can use Northwest (and Southeast) rooms. Kitchens find a compatible place in the Southeast and Northwest sectors, as a second option. Restrooms and washing areas are best avoided in the Northeast and Southwest areas.

Divine Habitations

Temples are normally based on the 64 module plan called *manduka mandala.* The Asana or 100 module plan is also considered. Beginning with the *Garbagriha* or Sanctum Sanctorum in the centre, a temple normally has several enclosures called *Prakara.*

These are based on certain rules of height, thickness and spacing of the enclosures that increase as they go out. A properly built temple generally has five enclosures but some go up to seven. The five enclosures, beginning from the innermost enclosure are *Antara Mandala, Antaranihara, Madhyamahara, Prakara* and *Mahamaryada.*

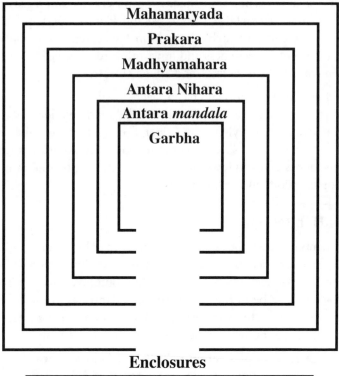

Fig. 01.02

Importance of the Main Door

The placement of the main door is extremely important. The four important zones for placing a main door in the four cardinal directions are:

- *Indra* (East)
- *Brihatakshata* (South)
- *Kusumandanta* (West)
- *Bhallata* (North)

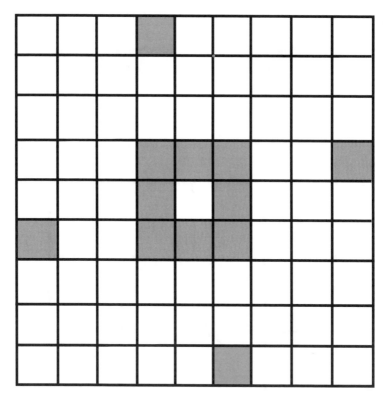

Door Positions

Fig. 01.03

Divide each side into nine parts. The exalted zone would be the fourth from your right as you face the building.

Avoid doors in the middle of the building. According to **Samarangna Sutradhara** a door in the middle indicates negative effects on the family. However, middle doors are approved for temples.

The main door has to be the biggest of all doors. **Manasara** suggests that the height of a door has to be atleast twice its width. **Brihat Samhita** and **Visvakarma Prakasha** prescribe a height thrice the width of the door. The main door has to be attractive, solid and massive and can be strengthened with the help of various metals.

The ancient seers of India saw life as one of total happiness that could be granted on all by Vastu and its practical application. Vastu creates contentment in one's life within a frame-work defined by one's *Prarabdha Karma*, which is indicated in the individual's horoscope. Based on certain *Dasas* and *Bhukthis*, various transits and aspects on the fourth and other houses, results vary.

Vastu and astrology are inter-related and inter-dependant. It is the synthesis and the integration of the information from the two areas that can ultimately help an individual. The fourth house considerations in one's horoscope are important.

		Lagna	Moon
	Rasi		
			Fourth House

The fourth house in a horoscope

Fig. 01.04

A study of the fourth house reveals houses, landed and ancestral properties, peace of mind, mother, home life, conveyances and general happiness. When judging the houses, one's analysis should not be merely literal but need to be knowledge based, experience and coupled with intuition. While studying the fourth house, some of the factors that need to be carefully considered are summarized below.

- Strength, aspects, conjunctions and position of the lord of the fourth house.

- Strength of the house itself

- Natural qualities of the house, of its lord and the planets in it or having aspects

- Yogas occurring in a particular house

- The exaltation or debilitation of the house lord

- The age, position, status and sex of the person

- The disposition of planets in a sign and the relationship of the house lord with the Sun.

- Operating Dashas and Bhukthis

- Transits of Saturn, Jupiter, Rahu and Mars.

The importance of horoscope comes into play at four stages of construction. They are:

1. Laying the foundation

2. Digging of the well, bore well or constructing the underground water tank.

3. Installing the main door or *Mahadwara* of the house

4. Entering the completed house

Energy Fields

Vastu refers to the form of construction of the house and the energies or force called into existence by the arrangements made and the materials used in the construction. The subtle results, effected by the energy interaction of the various materials, though not obvious to the naked eye do exist. Any malefic tendencies they may produce could harm the occupants of the house or building, and they need to be neutralized or counteracted. Jyotish Sastra provides certain remedial methods to minimize any negative trends indicated in the horoscope.

Correspondingly, Vastu Sastra also provides remedial methods to correct or to remove imbalance in the orientation and construction of a house or any other building. In summary, Vastu is also used to optimize the positive signals and reduce the negative indications shown in an individual's horoscope.

Our sages have said that neither destiny nor free will is absolute. As humans, our efforts need to be oriented towards getting the best out of destiny and free will so that one can have peace, happiness, health and adequate prosperity.

2

Orientations & Topography

THE ANCIENT masters of Vastu or Vedic architecture highlighted the importance of proper orientation. Orientation of a layout, site or building (residence or business) influences the dwellers in terms of living, education, physical and mental health, family relationships, finances and general welfare. The classical textbooks of Vastu identify different plans for varied applications. One of them known as *Peeta Mandala* consists of nine modules and identifies the primary elements water, fire, space and air in the four corners and earth in the center of the area.

Vayu **Air**		**Udaka** **Water**
	Prithvi **Earth**	
Akasha **Space**		**Agni** **Fire**

Fig. 02.01

It is said that the magnetic field runs North-South through the globe and the Sun gives life to the electromagnetic field in the East-West orientation. The ancients considered geo-graphical orientation, primarily based on the movement of the Sun. Electric current flows through the earth's molten core. When it rotates, a magnetic field is produced that extends into space.

The earth's magnetic center is generally inclined at about 11° from its axis of rotation. This means that magnetic North is 11° from the geographical North. Hence, when the compass orientation indicates a maximum tilt of 11°, the orientation can be taken to be in order. This tilt in magnetic orientation can be north or south depending whether it is the Northern progress of the Sun from Capricorn to Cancer (*Uttarayana*) or Southern progress of the Sun from Cancer to Capricorn (*Dakshinayana.*)

Distinguished teachers of *Sthapatya Veda* tell us that proper orientation can help in preventing possible chaos, conflict and failure. While creating a residential (house or apartment) layout, proper orientation of buildings and pathways to the cardinal directions helps in cross-ventilation and creates order and balance that is so indispensable for contentment and happiness. Once the properly oriented site or buildings are identified, the appropriate placement of doorways and windows in certain directions can add to the general welfare and happiness. Orientation can be in relation to sitting and sleeping arrangements.

Temple Orientation

The need for the creative and beneficial solar energies of the morning appear to be the basis for many of the temples to be oriented to the East. The ancient masters felt that proper orientation interfaced the powerful and subtle energies of humans, animals and buildings (*pindanda*) with the extensive energies coming from millions of universes (*brahmanda*.)

However, some temples are not oriented to the East. One of Lord Siva's manifestations, Lord Dakshinamurthi, is invariably oriented to the South. Ancients accorded special reverence to the Lord as the ultimate Guru or Teacher. He is said to be the embodiment of knowledge and destroyer of ignorance. He is the teacher of the sages and gods. Lord Dakshinamurthi, symbolizing a teacher par excellence, is shown in the temples in meditation with a snake (and a rosary) in one hand and fire in the other, signifying divine knowledge and enlightenment respectively. Temples were also oriented based on their proximity to mountains, lakes and roads. It is not uncommon to find a few temples of Siva, Vishnu and the mother goddess facing South, North and West with lakes and mountains nearby.

Building Orientation

Orientation to the North and East are traditionally acceptable. However, ancient treatises do not prohibit orientation to the South or West. Orientation of a site or building was also based on the surrounding topography and local weather conditions.

Astrological compatibility to certain directions are also integrated while selecting a specific site or building.

Dual Orientation

Possible effects of the various dual orientations are indicated below.

In the case of a dining room, class room, lecture hall or an auditorium (cultural or entertainment), an East-West orientation can be the first preference and North-South can be the second option, such that the youngsters face North or East and the elder members, the South or West. In a classroom, the students can face North or East and the teaching faculty can face South or West. Students who need to learn and assimilate all that is taught by the master's face east, the direction of sunrise and teachers who need to set their knowledge into the creative minds of the students face west, the direction of sunset. As for the teachers facing south, it is related to Lord Dakshinamurthi, the greatest of the teachers.

In the case of an entertainment auditorium, the performing artistes can orient to the South or West and the audience can face North or East. In the case of a marriage hall, the audience faces North or East. On the stage the couple and their parents can face east, if the audiences face north. They can face north, if the audiences face east. Consequently the priests and their assistants face South or West. In the case of a lecture auditorium, the speaker can face South or West and the audiences face North or East.

If the speaker on the dais faces south, various display related equipment's (overhead projectors, liquid crystal display or black / White board) can be to the Northwest and the speaker's microphone to the Northeast. When the speaker faces west, the display can be to the Southeast and the speaker's mike to the northeast.

Sleep

Sleep is necessary in keeping good health and one's body and soul together. Students and unmarried young men and women who are still in the process of building their careers can sleep with their heads to the East. It is considered that a current of electricity passing from one part of the body to the other part subdues all inflammation in that part of the body.

The earth's body is continuously magnetized by thermal energy produced by the Sun. When the Eastern part of the earth is heated, its Western part remains cold. Consequently, the thermal energy generated by the Sun travels over the surface of the earth from East to West.

Sage Markandeya

The celebrated sage Markandeya tells us that man becomes learned when he sleeps with his head to the East. It appears that the thermal energy helps in creating a comfortable environment when one sleeps with the head placed in the East. When the head is placed in the West, the flow of this energy creates possible disturbance to sleep resulting in some distress and confused thinking.

Sage Markandeya also tells us that man acquires strength and longevity by sleeping with his head to the South. When the current of thermal electricity passes from the East to the West, the earth becomes magnetized and its geographical North Pole, which is to the right hand side of the direction of current, becomes the magnetic North pole and its geographical South Pole being on the left-hand side of the same current, becomes the magnetic South Pole.

It has been proved by experiments that the human, body is capable of being magnetized and that it contains a large percentage of iron in the blood that circulates all through the body. As the feet are always in constant contact with the huge magnet (the earth) which exhibits the properties of North polarity, South polarity is induced in our feet and consequently North polarity is induced in the head.

The body enjoys good health because of the natural polarity being unaltered. On the other hand when the head is placed to the North, the natural polarity gets altered and affects the health. Let me reiterate that the ancients have approved of orientation to all the four cardinal directions — North, East, South and West. A proper orientation assures the qualitative life. Orientations to the angular directions are not recommended. Classical works identify certain orientations to certain attributes. Orientation to the Southeast generally points to constant fear, Southwest to quarrels and friction, Northwest to indiscrimination and Northeast to disturbance to or of progeny.

Elevations and Depressions

The ancient masters have also identified the elevations and depressions of a site as of great importance in the happiness or otherwise of the residents of a building. Uniformly level ground is approved and contributes to general happiness. Sites that are not level and have natural elevations and depressions such that the areas elevated to the South and West and slope down to the North and East respectively will assure natural rainwater and underground water to flow in a clockwise direction throughout the year.

Elevations and depressions can be artificially created too by constructing rock gardens in the South and the West and water areas — underground tanks, pools etc., in the North and East. The cumulative effect of directional orientation and elevation-depression are summarized below.

- Southeast elevation and Northwest depressions are positive.
- Northwest elevation and Southeast depressions are not desirable.
- Southwest elevations and Northeast depressions indicate financial stability and mature thinking.
- Elevations in the Northeast and depressions in the Southwest indicate ill-health and loss of money.
- West elevation and East depression indicate prosperity.
- East elevation and West depression point to loss of Wealth.
- South elevation and North depression point to gain of Wealth.
- North elevation and South depression indicate loss of wealth and ill-health.
- North and Northwest elevations and Southeast depressions indicate disease and ill-health.
- West and Northwest elevations and East and Southeast depressions indicate constant quarrels and enmity.
- Northeast and East elevations and Southwest and West depressions point to constant differences among family members.

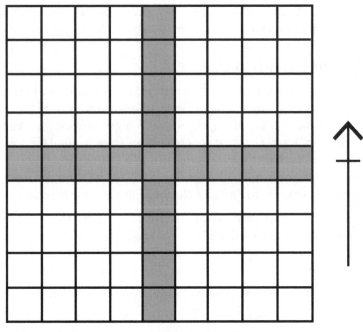

Orientation to cardinal directions

Fig. 02.02

- Northeast and North elevations and Southwest and South depressions indicate disharmony in the family.

- Similar indications are shown when Southeast is depressed and Southwest, Northwest, and Northeast are elevated.

- Northeast, Southeast and West elevated and Southwest depressed points to loss of grain.

- Southwest and Northeast elevated and Northwest and East depressed indicate unhappiness.

- Northeast, North and East elevated and the rest depressed indicate loss of money and imbalance of ethics.

Orientation and topography within and around any area are important aspects of Vastu. Towns and villages were planned such that the orientation of the streets and sites was to the cardinal directions and never to the angular or vidisha directions. Ancient masters formulated principles of Vastu based on observation, experience, intuition and wisdom.

Many of the arrived conclusions and the corresponding recommendations made by them are meant to be not only spiritually and materially beneficial to the individual but also to integrate the wellness of the individual with the well-being of the society.

The great men and women of learning saw the domino effect that integrates the individual, family, society and the humanity-at-large. Vastu provides many simple but effective guidelines, so that human effort is always oriented and directed towards the goal of making the world a better place to live in.

3

Foundations
&
Soil Evaluation

I HAVE, over a period of several years (in my earlier books) tried to present information on various aspects of house building vis-a-vis the great science of Indian Architecture, Vastu. We have tried to understand the plans of the ancients referred to as mandala; we have tried to understand different types of houses referred to as sala houses; we have tried to understand the various rooms in a residential building, referred to as *Manushyalaya*. Apart from other aspects of Vastu we have also tried to understand something of temple architecture, referred to as *Devalaya*.

We have more or less talked about the structures above the ground level (superstructures.) Have our ancients not spoken about below the ground constructions? Have our ancients not spoken of the foundations and basements? Do we not need to understand their concept of laying a foundation ?

Yes, they have spoken about foundations in chapters referred to as *Garbha Vinyasa*. *Manasara*, *Samarangana Sutradhara* and *Mayamata*, the repositories of Vastu Vidya have specifically spoken of the importance of proper foundations for the stability of structures.

They tell us the excavation has to go down up to the surface that is hard or where water is found. Here, we may, for a while, consider one of the modern methods of site exploration, which is termed as test pit method. Here, a square pit is dug up to a depth at which hard soil is located. The ancients also mentioned depth in terms of being as high as the basement.

Foundation is described as the solid ground that is prepared to take the load of the superstructure. The importance of a proper foundation is highlighted when we see huge superstructures that are under construction suddenly collapsing. A foundation is required to distribute and bear the load of the superstructure, to have hard surface for concreting and masonry work and other factors like distribution of non-uniform loads, prevention and minimizing cracks, providing lateral stability for structure against natural forces like rain, earthquake, wind etc.

The term foundation is a common term that is quite familiar to anyone associated with building construction. It is the ground or base on which the structure rests. The foundation in the case of building is partly or wholly below the surface of the ground. It is a simple engineering fact that any kind of loads (weight etc.), whether from the roof, floor or any other part of a structure ultimately need to be transferred to Mother Earth.

Who else but Mother Earth is capable of fully and comfortably absorbing the load inside her limitless belly? The total load on the foundation primarily results from the "dead" load (weight of roof, walls, floors, furniture, etc.) of the structure and the "live" load (wind, snow and hail) that is often imposed by Nature. The impressive and imposing live load applied by Nature on a structure is a constant reminder to humanity that in the final count, man is merely another creation of God.

In the case of a simple or ordinary residential construction, the engineer calculates the bearing or compressive load imposed by each layer of foundation on the next layer of the foundation. Based on the intensity of load applied on the surface area, each successive layer is gradually larger than the previous layer contained in the foundation. The idea is that ultimately the intensity of the load transfer should be such that the ground below can take the compressive or bearing load without the soil or earth being overstressed or disturbed. The engineer may consider the simple or complex foundation to be merely made of mortar, bricks, concrete, stones, steel etc.

The Vedic heritage considers the foundation as more than a physical construction or structure. It is indeed an interface that links the man-made superstructure with the divine Mother Earth; the foundation is considered as a symbolic homage from man to Mother Earth. The engineering aspects of various types of foundations and their designs are discussed in many of the classical engineering textbooks and other references. Our interest in foundation is more than its physical structure. Our ancient masters through the medium of Vastu Shastra have explained the spiritual and other theological aspects related to foundations.

While modern civil engineers visit sites and inspect them from the viewpoint of foundation, our ancients also stressed the need to examine the site. They spoke of tests that checked on the strength of the soil before construction began. One of these tests was to dig the soil the previous night and then fill up the pit with the dug-up soil. Depending on how the pit was filled, the soil was declared as fit, moderate and totally unfit. If we carefully observe this simple test of soil strength that our ancients spoke of, we will be surprised that modern engineers too speak of soil testing for assessing their strength and suitability for construction.

Filling the dug-up pit with water and observing the fall in the water level also tested the strength of the soil. The soil conditions were also checked by other simple experiments like ploughing the soil, which indicated the soil composition in the upper crust of the site. The ancients felt that the presence of animal wastes like bones and hair indicated unsuitable soil conditions. The soil condition was also said to be bad if the presence of vermin and termites was noticed. These made the soil hollow.

After testing the suitability of the soil, modern engineering science also speaks of the depths of excavation required for laying a foundation for the superstructure. While speaking of the excavation, our ancients have spoken of the depth of foundation being equal to *Kaya*. *Kaya* is referred to as the height of the master and is equal to *Vyama* or the stretch of his hands.

The depth of the excavation was filled by seven kinds of earth from rivers, mountains, anthills, crab-holes, sea-shores, hills and from near a cowshed. The sides were made of *ishtika* (baked bricks) and *sila* (stones.) Water was poured on each layer of soil, sand and pieces of stones and stamped upon by elephants to make the foundation closely pressed and hardened. The ancients spoke of deposits being placed in the excavation. These included various crops and roots of certain flowers in the four cardinal directions and the four angular directions.

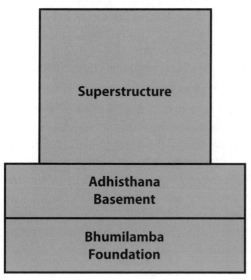

The base (*adhishtana*) is to be built on the foundation and is equal to the height of the foundation. This means that the structure is built at a height from the ground, taking into consideration the period of time over which the ground level could go up but yet the *adhishtana* prevents rainwater, sewerage etc., entering the compound or house structure.

Superstructure

Adhisthana
Basement

Bhumilamba
Foundation

Fig. 03.01

Mayamata speaks of fourteen types of *Adhishtanas* — *Padabandha, Ugrabandha, Pratikrama, Padma Kesara, Pushpa Pushkala, Sribandha, Mancha Bandha, Srikanta, Shreni Bandha, Padma Bandha, Vapra Bandha, Kapota Bandha, Prati Bandha* and kalasa. These are described with different heights, each being divided into several parts. For the whole structure to be harmonious, the ancients spoke of the base being proportionate to the building. The height of the building was also related to being half the size of the pillars or less by 1/6th, 1/7th or 1/8th.

While speaking about the pillars, our ancients have fixed the height and diameter of the pillars. Talking about 12-storied temples, they prescribe the pillar a height of eight and a half hastas (12 feet 9 inches.) The width of a pillar is given as twenty-eight angulas (1 foot 9 inches.) The foundation stone is not to be laid down if the master's wife is pregnant (6th month onwards.)

Concluding, we can infer that our ancients were very aware of every aspect of building construction. They were aware of not only the modern principles of engineering but also of the subtle cosmic energies that radiate in and around a human being with reference to his place of habitation. As I always say, they just wanted us to go with natural laws and vibe with nature to make life better and more meaningful.

4

Relevance To Corporate Houses

IN RECENT times, there has been a global rise in the importance of Vastu in not only in our residences where general health and happiness are of paramount importance but also in our commercial buildings where proper inflow and outflow of funds reign supreme.

Besides the structural and architectural beauty, there are other aspects that Vastu looks into, to make the building, the ambience and environment conducive for successful corporate meetings. They felt that the land and the structures on the land were living organisms, the land being the womb (of mother earth) and the structure, the seed. Their well-being was so necessary for a healthy offspring — the health and happiness of the residents.

The ancients have spoken of various plans (*mandalas*) and have recognized the positions of the primary elements of nature (*Panchamahabhoota*) in the plan referred to as *Peeta*. The proper placement of these Primary elements, viz., Water (*Udaka*), Fire (*Dahana* or *Agni*), Air or Wind (*Vayu*), Ether or Space (*Gagana*) and Earth (*Prithvi*) can assist in proper exchange of ideas between business collaborators for successful corporate/business meetings. They have also spoken of the various energies coming from the different directions.

General Topography

General topography around the building can conform to certain simple Vastu requirements.

Ideally, there should be other buildings and/or physical blocks etc., to the South and West as defense from the southwest energies that are generally not supportive. To the North and East there can exist water areas and open spaces which can add to proper communication skills so very necessary for good business. While selecting your site avoid areas where several roads converge on your site.

Roads or corridors or passages jutting into your office/workplace/ structure need to be carefully considered too. When they pierce certain directions, business is prone to financial and/or compatibility disturbances. It would be good to steer clear of South of Southwest and West of Southwest roads, corridors, passages. Disturbances can be minimized by proper landscaping and placing the right yantras (consecrated copper pieces with specific designs on them.)

Avoid selection of a structure/site that is clubbed between two bigger structures/sites. Have the building oriented to the cardinal directions only. As far as feasible shun dissimilar floor levels. However, if this becomes inevitable, settle for elevated heights in the South and West and lower heights in the North and East.

Avoid triangle and other irregular shapes for your building. Walls that orient 90° to each other are recommended. Plainly put, rectangular structures are recommended. Our ancients compared a building with several storeys to a musical instrument. A *thambura, veena, violin, guitar, sitar* or any stringed instrument that is meant to give rhythm and music have the distance between successive strings reducing as they go up.

Height of each floor should be lesser than the previous floor. In fact **Brihat Samhita** suggests one-twelfth of the previous floor height as the reducing unit.

Importance of Mahadwara (Main Door)

When building or buying your corporate or business premises give enough thought to the main entry and the main door. As I have pointed out repeatedly in my earlier writings, the following openings based on the *Paramasayika Mandala* (81 module plan) are suggested for main doors. On the Eastern side, the second, third and fourth modules (from North) called *Parjanya, Jayanta* and *Indra* are the exalted door openings. On the Southern side (from East), you have the fourth module, *Brihatakshata*. You have *Kusumadanta* and *Varuna*, the fourth and fifth modules respectively on the West side (from the South). On the northern side, you have the exalted doorways in the third, fourth and fifth modules respectively called *Mukhya, Bhallata* and *Soma*. However, I do not recommend doors on the fifth module for residential or business houses.

Arranging the Interiors

Let us now look into the interiors. Apart from general considerations of proper lighting and ventilation, proper placement of personnel and their furniture based on some simple guidelines of Vastu are recommended.

The Southwest or South of the structure can be reserved for the Chairman, Director or the General Manager. You can have your seating in the Southwest sector of your room facing North or East and arrange your desk in such a way that you sit on your chair walking from the Northeast of your chamber. Important documents, cash and other assets that need to be taken care off can be in the southwest (at a higher level) or Northwest (at a lower level) of your rooms. Files that need to be attended to by your subordinates can be set aside in the Northwest or Southeast of your room for swift clearance.

The North and Northeast sectors are ideal for people managing the financial records. Within that sector allotted for accounts section, the financial or accounts manager can be seated in the Southwest facing east. Rest of the staff mainly concerned with writing of the accounts can face north.

As the center of an area relates to the *brahmasthana* or the place of zero ego and total awareness, conference rooms where serious discussions between the business partners or between the management and the labor takes place can be located there. Where nothing much can be done, this central area can be kept totally clean and the better way of doing this is to place an idol of God or a *Shikara* Pyramid in the exact center. The Northeast sector of the office is also recommended for conference rooms. The Chairman's seat can be placed such that he faces North or East and the other people can face each other in the East-West axis. Conference rooms can have their walls painted white or lighter shades of green.

Generators, inverters, computers, transformers, etc. find a habitable place in the Southeast sector. With this principle in mind, the various rooms of the chairman, directors, managers and staff can be designed so that the southeast corners of the respective rooms. This sector is also ideal for having the kitchens and pantry. Kitchen and dining areas can have lighter shades of orange on their walls.

General lounges where employees just relax for lunch and other non-business activities can be planned in the Northwest sectors of the office. Toilets can also be located in the Northwest sectors. The Northwest of the site can have the office garden too. Business merchandise that needs to be marketed also finds the Northwest sector compatible for their storage. Relaxing areas can have walls with soft or dark hues of blue.

Generally speaking have your doors on the North of Northeast, East of Northeast, West of Northwest and South of Southeast. Let not your door directly face a staircase. If it does, make use of plants to carefully camouflage the area and this helps diffuse the negative energies that barge into your doorway. Have the doors opening inside in the clockwise direction. Avoid door closers that forcefully activate extreme energy into your room/office. Normal curtains should be good enough. As mentioned in the earlier part of this write-up, avoid passages jutting into your doors.

Avoid untidiness at the entrance of your room/office. As the ancients put it, avoid a *dwara shoola* (obstruction to your door.) Avoid sitting under beams. If you have to, conceal the beams with false ceilings. Mezzanine floors can be in the South West and Southwest sectors of the building/office. General administrative staff that need to face each other can best be seated facing East-West axis. Concluding, our ancients have handed over the secrets in the form of Vastu to make our life more meaningful. By properly planning your office structure / furniture as per Vastu, you can regulate the energies, cosmic and human, to make your business prosper. Vastu optimizes the positive signals and reduces the impact of the negative signals indicated by our astrological charts.

5

Senior Citizens
&
Old Age Homes

THE STUDY of Vastu Sastra and related Vedic subjects has fascinated me for a number of years. The benefits of proper Vast planning are far reaching. When it is applied to educational institutions, business complexes, satellite towns, public buildings, residential dwellings etc., it will significantly enhance over a period of time the total quality of life of the society-at-large.

I have always wondered and worried over the fate of many elderly people who have led their earlier lives well and over the years, made a number of sacrifices so that their children have good education and quality life.

Unfortunately, these days, many aged parents who are at the twilight of their lives are subjected by their very own grown-up children to ridicule and extreme humiliation. The children who received great love and affection from their parents and are now grown-up reciprocate, if at all, very little affection but a lot of contempt for their aged parents. In these troubled times, the senior citizens are virtually homeless and with great difficulty, have to fend for themselves. Years back, the twilight years of the parents were torch lights of affection, gratitude and love. Now the twilight years are more like torched lives.

Yet, in the midst of such a situation in society, it is quite heartening to note that quite a few *Vriddhashramas* or Old Age Homes are slowly coming to the rescue of the elderly people. I have also pondered, over and over again, on the rather helpless seniors having to stay in old age homes. I feel that if our builders, engineers, contractors and architects apply the principles of Vastu, they can build not only a nice and comfortable home for the elder members of the society, but also be instrumental in helping their health and creating some happiness to them. In addition, they will contribute and assist in establishing — a cleaner and saner society!

Joint Families

Not too long ago, we had a very strong joint family system. Those days as the children grew up into adults and the parents into senior citizens, the responsibility of taking care of the seniors automatically shifted to the children. Senior citizens were (and are) priceless to the nation because of their wisdom, experience and rational approach to problem solving. Seniors shared their experience and wisdom with their sons and daughters.

Members of the family felt that grandparents were best suited to take care of the young children, inculcating human and moral values in them. It is pertinent to note here that most houses built in the earlier decades had invariably central courtyards (*Brahmastana*) and these areas were free from any habitation and were always open to the skies. It was not uncommon to see a joint family that had thirty plus people consisting of grandparents, grand uncles, children, nephews and grandchildren affectionately and lovingly staying in one single house and happily eating food prepared in a common kitchen!

Unfortunately, today the joint family system is getting rarer and virtually extinct. Young couples in rural areas and towns have begun to migrate to the cities and other countries in search of improved employment opportunities, knowing fully well that they are living in very competitive world. The youth, though not disrespectful to their elders, may not express their affection properly, thus creating an atmosphere of misunderstanding. While the earlier young generation considered taking care of the elders their bounden duty, the present younger generations do not feel the same way. Many times, some feel that their elderly parents tend to place unrealistic demands on them. Some young people feel that the elders in the family keep on harping on their own 'good old days' rather than realizing the times have changed, for better or worse, for them and their children. While elders may feel that their sons and daughters have to refrain from excessive spending, the modern adult does not want any 'interference' in his dealings, earnings and spending from his parents. These and many other reasons have contributed to the widening of the generation gap, gradually leading to the break-up of the traditional joint family system. As a consequence of such changes in society, there is more focus today on the necessity and importance of old age homes.

Location and Design

Senior citizen homes that are meant to provide solace to the elders should have a calm, pollution-free environment. A proper location is important. They can be situated in quiet idyllic surroundings or in an urban area where they have quick access to facilities of the city. Of course, topography is an important consideration. It's ideal to have mountains and high-rise buildings in the South and West; fauna and foliage in the North and East; Water areas like ponds, lakes, water reservoirs in the North and Northeast; electrical transformers etc., in the Southeast, South and East and gardens in the Northwest, North and West.

N

Women Hospital Staff Recreation Sports	Women	Medicines, Short term treatment, Meditation room
Recreation Sports	Verandah · Temple · Verandah (Verandah sides)	Medicines, Medical Accessories Active Sports
Couples Men Adminstrator's Office	Couples Men Administrator's Office	Active Sports

Fig. 05.01

They can be of dormitory type, independent rooms or cottages depending on the social and economic status of those who will live in these homes.

The rooms can be well-ventilated and can be housed in the ground level as much as possible, so that all facilities are easily available at one level for the seniors. If upper floors are built, sloping ramps and lifts will assist in easy movement of seniors requiring wheel chairs. The ramps can be done in such a way that they go up clock-wise and *slope down* to the East and North directions only. The toilets and bathrooms can have rough flooring so that the elders do not slip. If there are attached bathrooms they can be to the Northwest or Southeast of the rooms and if they are independent blocks, they can be located in the Northwest or Southeast of the building. Appropriate railings can be provided for support. South and Southwest blocks of the site or building will be ideal for couples and men and North and Northwest blocks for women. A few rooms can be set apart for people requiring short-term medical treatment. These can be in the Northeast of the site or building. Recreation rooms for the elders can be in the North, West and Northwest of the building.

Administrator's Office

Old age homes generally have an office that consists of an administrator who is responsible for proper running of the home. He can be housed in a South or Southwest room of the building. The staff at these facilities include clerks, cashier, accountant, nursing staff, attenders, maids and cooks. If they are provided quarters in the home, they can all be placed in the Northwest of the building or housed in the Northwest of the site.

Medicines and Medical Accessories

All medicines and medical accessories that maybe needed for treatment of the residents can be stored in the East and Northeast of the site or rooms. Transport vehicles can be in the Northwest sectors of the site. Well-maintained old age homes generally have recreational facilities such as televisions and video players in the North, West and Northwest, and libraries for reading newspapers and books in the North, East and Northeast. Facilities for active sports such as tennis, table tennis, and squash can be provided in the South, East and Southeast sectors of the site.

Medical camps can be organized where leading doctors are invited to diagnose and treat the residents periodically. They can be taken out for small walks in the morning and evening. Seniors, suffering from illness, can be kept in separate blocks in the Northeast of the home and special attention provided to them. The atmosphere has to be conducive for their mental and physical happiness. Apart from providing the basic requirements like food, clothing, and shelter etc., the motto of properly managed old age homes should be to provide the senior citizens a feeling of warmth and make them feel wanted.

Summing up

Senior citizen homes that are built in conformance with the various aspects of Vastu indicated here will bring some happiness and contentment to senior citizens. The following basic guidelines need to be considered for selecting the site and for locating the various living areas in the building.

- Select land that slopes towards North or East.
- The land selected should orient to the cardinal (North, South, East and West) directions.
- Thoroughly till the soil and remove any nails, bones and other dirt.
- Rectify the site to a rectangle or square by building a wall around, such that the angles are at 90°.
- Divide the site into 81 equal modules or cells.
- The outermost region, which is the paisacha Zone, is to be left alone.
- The next two zones, which are the Manushya and Daiva, can be used for the construction of various rooms etc.
- The central nine squares can be the open courtyard consisting of the garden and open space for the seniors to sit and relax.
- Prayers can be held in the Northeast sectors of the building or site. Of course, the ideal place 'will be the central courtyard or the Brahmastana that is normally referred to as the place of zero ego and total awareness.
- The Southeast can be the kitchen.
- The South, West, East and North can contain the rooms for the elderly people.
- The South and Southwest can have the administrative office of the home.

- The meditation center and the medicine room can be in the Northeast and East.

- The door into the building can be in one of the exalted zones.

- The dining area can be near the kitchen.

- If cows are maintained, they can be tied in the Northwest of the site.

- Attached toilets can be to the Northwest or Southeast of the rooms.

- The Southwest rooms can accommodate couples, South and East can accomodate men and the North and West rooms, the women.

- A well or under-ground tank (sump) can be dug in the North of Northeast.

- The courtyard can have a verandah all around for movement from room to room.

- Ramps and stairs into the first floors can go upward in the clock-wise direction.

- Recreational activity rooms can be in the Northwest and Southeast and libraries in the Northeast and East of the building or site.

- Short term treatment rooms for the inmates can be in the Northeast sector.

Architectural and engineering aspects, especially from the viewpoint of comfort and convenience of the senior people, have to be taken care of.

Strong foundations, minimum number of stairs, no obstacles either in the rooms or in the courtyard or in the compound, large windows to allow fresh air to seep in and not to forget a well-trained staff and administrator capable of understanding the seniors hearts all add up to make the old age home a haven for the senior citizens!

6

Buying An Apartment

OVER THE last few years, we have seen the growing awareness of the importance of Vastu to contemporary times. In our country (India), most people build, buy or rent a residence/commercial building only after they are satisfied that it is in agreement with certain Vastu guidelines. The last few years have also seen that more and more apartments – both residential and business – are being built for reasons of convenience, security and other factors. Many of the apartments that have been carefully scrutinized by me have not passed the "litmus test" of Vastu. I wish to deal with Vastu aspects covering apartments from both perspectives — one from the viewpoint of the builder and the other from the view point of the buyer or the tenant.

General Requirements

Generally speaking, apartments become sales-worthy because of certain reasons. Many questions crop up before one decides to buy or rent an apartment.

- Is the apartment building or block accessible on all the sides through proper roads?
- Do the apartments get enough natural light?
- Is the overall area in proper shape and is any work needed to make the apartment more habitable?

- Are there enough complexes, hospitals, restaurants, schools and colleges, banks and other financial institutions in proximate distance to the apartments?

- Do the apartments have enough water pressure so that water is properly delivered?

- Are there a number of electrical outlets, and where they are exactly placed. How big are the water heaters?

- Is there enough closet space or if extra storage is needed.

- What utilities is the individual buyer or tenant responsible for?

- Are pets allowed?

- Are there restrictions on the number of pets?

- How is the television reception?

- Will one need a cable network?

- Is there clear information covering any existing wear or damage or a penalty for breaking the lease?

- Do the amenities include linen, cooking equipment and flatware, microwave oven, family size refrigerator with icemaker, dishes, dishwasher, color cable TV, central heat and air conditioning, telephone, ocean front balcony, large swimming pool, lighted tennis courts, shuttle board courts, clubhouse, 24-hour security, on premise laundry facilities, etc.?

Vastu Requirements

- Are all these conveniences, luxuries and comforts enough to make the individual and the family happy?

- Will they also provide mental peace?

Our ancients felt, that apart from material conveniences and comforts, the understanding of the importance of Vastu and applying it in the construction of a structure goes a long way in promoting contentment, reasonable happiness and mental peace.

We will review, relative to Vastu guidelines, a few apartments that have already been constructed and are occupied.

Single-bedroom Apartments

A and B are two single-bedroom apartments ready for habitation. Let us compare and see which of the two apartments pass the test (requirements) of Vastu. The main door for both the apartments is on the south.

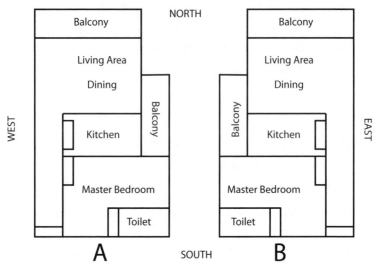

The kitchens for both the apartments are in the *Brahmastana* or the central areas of the apartments.

1. 'A' has a south of southwest main door. ✗
   'B' has a south of southeast main door. ✓

2. 'A' has a southeast master bedroom. ✗
   'B' has a southwest master bedroom. ✓

3. 'A' has a northwest extension. ✗
   'B' has a northeast extension. ✓

4. 'A' has a west door for the bedroom. ✗
   'B' has an east door for the bedroom. ✓

5. 'A' bedroom has water to its southeast. ✗
   'B' bedroom has Water to its southwest. ✗

6. 'A' kitchen is to the north- west of the bedroom. ✓

   'B' kitchen is to the northeast of the bedroom. ✗

7. 'A' has the toilet in the southeast. ✓

   'B' has the toilet in the south-west. ✗

The Vastu test or evaluation is based on the available options. Apartment A 'passes only 2 out of 7 requirements and obtains a net percentage of 28. Apartment 'B' on the other, meets 4 out of 7 requirements and obtains a percentage of 57. Therefore, the Vastu test indicates that Apartment 'B' scores over Apartment A.'

'C' and 'D' are two Vastu approved single-bedroom apartments.

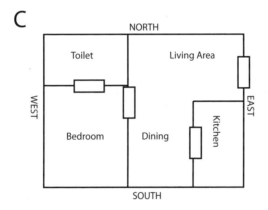

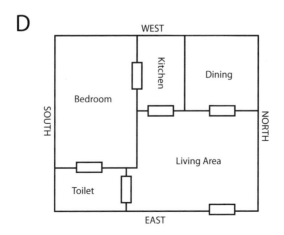

Double Bedroom Apartments

'E' and 'F' are two double-bedroom apartments ready for occupation. Let us compare and see which of the two apartments pass the test of Vastu.

The main doors for both the apartments are on the north.

1. 'E' has a north of northwest main door. ✗
   'F' has a north of northeast main door. ✓

2. 'E' has a southeast master bedroom. ✗
   'F' has a southwest master bedroom. ✓

3. 'E' has a northeast extension. ✓
   'F' has a northwest extension. ✗

4. 'E' has a west door for the master bed room. ✗
   'F' has an east door for the bedroom. ✗

5. 'E' has another bedroom in the northeast . ✓
   'F' has another bedroom in the northwest. ✓

6. 'E' - kitchen is in the southeast sector. ✓
   'F' - kitchen is in the south- west sector. ✗

7. 'E' - master bedroom has the toilet in the northeast. ✗
   'F' - master bedroom has the toilet in the northwest. ✓

The evaluation is based on the above.

Apartment 'E' passes 3 out of 7 Vastu requirements and obtains a net percentage of 43 while Apartment 'F' passes 4 out of 7 requirements and obtains a percentage of 57. Therefore, between the two, 'F' scores over 'E'. The northeast room can be used as a study room or as a bedroom for youngsters and elderly people.

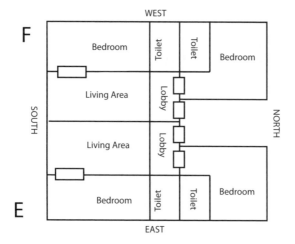

'G' and 'H' are two-bed room apartments. 'G' scores over 'H'

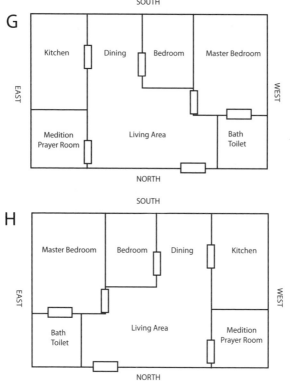

Three-Bedroom Apartments

'I' and 'J' are two three-bedroom apartments ready for occupation. Let us compare and see which of the two apartments pass the test of Vastu.

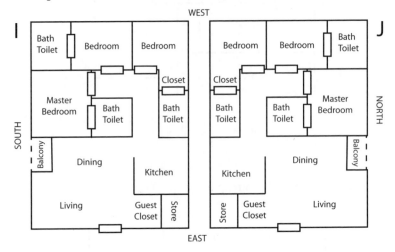

1. 'I' has an east of northeast main door ✓

   'J' has a south of south- east main door. ✗

2. 'I 'has a South of Southwest master bedroom. ✓

   'J' has a North of Northwest master bedroom. ✗

3. 'I' has a North of Northwest door for the master bedroom. ✓

   'J' has a South of Southwest door for the master bedroom. ✓

4. 'I' has one more bedroom in the West and another bedroom in the Northwest. ✓
   'J' has one more bedroom in the West and another in the Southwest. ✓

5. 'I' kitchen is in the Northeast sector. ✗

   'J' kitchen is in the Southeast sector. ✓

6. 'I' master room has the toilet to its Northeast. ✗

   'J' master room has the toilet to its Southeast. ✓

The evaluation is based on the options considered above. Apartment 'I' and Apartment 'J' get equal marks. Both pass. With the interiors done properly, the percentage can increase considerably.

7

Constructing Apartments

NOW, what are the various Vastu guidelines that the builder of an apartment has to take care of? What are the essential factors that he needs to look into before actual construction begins?

- Select a site that does not slope downwards to the south and/or west.
- Select a site that does not have water areas to its south and west.
- Plot the *Paramasayika* (81 modules) plan on the site and identify the central area relating to the Brahmastana (9 modules.)
- Draw the plan of the total construction that keeps the central area free from habitation.
- Always have the center of the total apartment block either to the southwest or northeast of the sital center.
- Make out the plans of the individual blocks as detailed earlier.
- Avoid staircases in the central area of the total apartment block.
- Avoid having the main entries into the site from the *south or west of southwest.*

In addition to the various factors indicated above, one need to take note of the following aspects:

- Never, ever have the main doors to the east of southeast, west or south of southwest and north of northwest of any apartment.

- The permitted main or inner doors are east or north of northeast, south of southeast and west of northwest.

- Never, ever have the water areas and cooking areas in the center of the apartment.

- As far as possible, design or plan apartments that are more or less rectangular without protrusions in any direction.

- Let the primary consideration be to allow natural light and ventilation from all the four sides, primarily north, east, south and west in that order.

The following general guidelines in respect of room locations in apartments can perhaps give some happiness and contentment to the residents.

- Single bedroom apartments can be in south or west and living areas in the north or east.

- Double bedroom apartments can have rooms in the south and west and living areas in the north and east.

- Three bedroom apartments can either have rooms in the south, West and east with living area in the north or rooms in the south, north and west with living area in the east.

- Four and multiple bedroom apartments can have rooms in all the four directions.

- The central spaces for bigger apartments can be living rooms for the family.

Concluding, our ancients have given us enough scope to regulate our lives by proper habitation. We just need to apply them carefully.

8

Colour Therapy

THIS chapter high lights the importance of colours with special reference to health. While one must consult a medical doctor when one has any kind of health problem, Vastu through the use of various colours will complement this human effort to get well. The Sun, often referred to as the royal planet, so necessary for sustaining human and other life, receives great importance

The Sun's rays are said to cure various illnesses and we know that sun-bathing is a common feature in the western world. The Sun's rays are effectively red (orange to be precise) in colour. The ancient texts identify each planet with certain colours and certain directions as given in Table 08.01.

Sun	Moon	Mars	Mercury	Jupiter
Copper Red Orange	White	Blood Red	Green	Gold or Bright Yellow
East	Northwest	South	North	Northeast
	Venus	**Saturn**	**Rahu**	**Ketu**
	Rainbow (mixture of all the colors)	Black (Blue)	Ultra-Violet	Infrared
	Southeast	West	Southwest	

Table 08.01

Table 08.02 identifies rulership of each planet over certain areas of the body. Colours can be hot or cold. Red, orange, yellow and infra-red are hot colours. Blue, indigo, violet and ultra-violet are said to be cold colours. Colours like orange, red and yellow are known as advancing colours and can make a room look smaller. Purple, blue, violet and green are known as receding colours and make a room look bigger than it is.

Sun	Moon	Mars	Mercury
Heart	Glands, lymphatic system sympathetic system, breasts and digestive juices	Voluntary muscular system	Brain, nerves, involuntary muscular tissues, lungs and power of locomotion
Jupiter	**Venus**	**Saturn**	
Liver, kidneys and pancreas	Generative organs, ovaries, kidneys, venous system, harmonic and the lumbar region.	Skeletal bones and spleen	

Table 08.02

Green rays impart strength to the human body and are also said to effectively reduce fevers like typhoid and other ailments arising due to heat. Inflammatory eye diseases are also said to respond to green rays. Green is cooling and is Mercury's colour. Earth, which is one of the primary elements, is said to be green. Green cures constant high fevers. Green can act as a sedative and help in alleviating sleeplessness. It builds muscle and tissue and is an effective therapy for asthma, high blood pressure, back disorders, piles, heart troubles, blood pressure, ulcers, cancer, headache, neuralgia and flu.

Blue rays are said to reside in all cavities of the human body and in the brain. The colour blue is said to be effective in curing whooping cough. It is said to be a cure for mental depression, sinus and underweight. It is an effective therapy for baldness, painful menstruation, eye inflammation, itching, hysteria, throat troubles, laryngitis, goiter, sore throat, hoarseness, teething fevers, scarlet fever, typhoid, cholera, plague, small pox, chickenpox, measles, apoplexy, hysteria, epilepsy, palpitations, stress, itches, toothaches, headache, nervous diseases and insomnia .

Indigo rays are cooling in nature and are a general tonic for good health. Indigo is deep blue and is the colour of the primary element water. Indigo rays are said to remove sterility in women and are sometimes beneficial in cases of insanity, fever, tuberculosis, etc. Indigo is said to cure eczema, differences between fighting couples, infertility, eye troubles, ear and voice complaints, facial paralysis, lung diseases, pneumonia, bronchitis, whooping cough, asthma, deafness, infantile convulsions, mental complaints, delirium and insanity.

Yellow rays are necessary for the thermal equilibrium of the human body. Those notable to do sustained work are said to benefit from yellow rays. These rays are hot in nature. Yellow is an effective therapy for constipation, eczema, flatulence, rheumatism, stomach troubles, indigestion, liver troubles, diabetes, blind piles, skin troubles, leprosy, and nervous exhaustion.

Orange rays are said to be effective in sanity and constant movement of a person from place to place, talking and thinking too much, rheumatic heart condition, sensitiveness to sound, light and smell, too much of bowel movements, anxiety and restlessness, heart injuries, heart palpitation, high blood pressure, heart inflammation, bleeding and piles, vomiting of blood, tuberculosis, delirium, female epilepsy, spasms and convulsions, over activity of nerves, anemia etc. Orange cures hemorrhoids and diarrhea and insomnia. Orange is also an effective therapy for chronic asthma, phlegmatic fevers, bronchitis, wet cough, gout, chronic rheumatism, and inflammation of kidneys, gall stones, cessation of menstruation, epilepsy, cholera, and mental debility. Orange is a combination of red and yellow and is a positive force.

Red rays are said to cure coma, pain in body, sinus, pain in knee joints and is a cure for corpulence, ailments of blood stream, anemia, physical debility, colds, circulatory deficiencies, paralysis, moronic cases and infantile paralysis. Violet rays are said to cure incessant and profuse bleeding, cancer, pain in knee joints, varicose veins. It is an effective therapy for nervous and mental disorders, neurosis, neuralgia, sciatica, scalp diseases, epilepsy, cerebro spinal cramps, rheumatism, tumors, kidney bladder weakness and venous blood. Walls can be painted and furniture, carpets, linen, upholstery and clothes can also incorporate colours. Colored curtains and carpets properly selected can strengthen the areas meant for certain activities.

For instance blue in the bedroom is recommended for good sleep. Green in the study room and office room is ideal for concentration and white and cream in prayer and living rooms enhance spiritual awareness and general thoughts. Orange in the dining area is recommended for good digestion. White is also excellent in rooms where you have elderly, invalid and sick patients.

Summing up, colours can make your rooms and your life aesthetic. Colours can excite you, depress you and delight you. Colours can remedy trouble spots. They can harmonize your living spaces. They can better/bitter your relationships. They can act as therapy for your elements. Each colour works individually and collectively.

Life is colour and colour is health. Proper usage of colours in our buildings, furniture, carpets, linen, curtains, floor and roof tiles, clothes and interfacing colour therapy with planets vis-to-vis their ruler ships and identification with directions as indicated above can help in better health.

9

Dwellings & Security

WE HAVE seen in the earlier pages, articles on various aspects of Vastu and its application to different areas or fields of modern architecture and engineering constructions.

In this chapter, we will look at some of the engineering or construction aspects of ancient forts and their strengthening for security. These remarkable historical forts contain many magnificent cities. Many of these forts and cities were damaged and destroyed over the centuries. Yet, there are still many forts that remind us of the glorious civilization of India and its great contribution to mankind. It is no surprise that Vastu was an integral part of the ancient forts and every construction that was contained within them. The study of the architecture and construction of these forts will immensely benefit us even today. Deep within them are embedded many practical aspects of Vastu. These forts, even if some of them are damaged, are still the living embodiments of the various principles of Vastu that we have inherited from the Vedic period.

Town Planning

Samarangana Sutradhara, the magnum opus of the science of Vastu, mentions 34 streets being laid in a town. These included the central streets called *Raja Marga*, the main streets called *Maharathya*, the smaller streets called *Yana Marga*, the bigger streets along the boundary of the town called *Ghanta Marga* that were as wide as the *Raja Marga* and the footpaths that were called *Jangha Pathas*.

Importance of Fortification

While speaking about the towns and palaces, the ancient books of Vastu have also identified the importance of making them secure by fortification. While the interiors of the towns were beautified with a host of flower bearing trees, the exteriors in a way were fortified with thorny bushes taking into consideration provision of free air, profuse sunshine and planting of trees. Fortification or strengthening was an integral part of town planning. Several ways of fortification for towns and palaces in them have been mentioned. *Rajaveshma* and *Rajanivesha* which refer to the residential quarters of kings and their families were a necessary and an important part of the development of a town or city. The royal palace was by and large positioned to the West of the Central area and oriented to the North. The position corresponds to the *Mitra* division of the *Mandooka* or 64 module plan.

Royal Palace

Manasara refers to the royal palace as *Rajaharmya* and identifies them by their size and relates to nine classes of kings —- *Sarvabhauma or Chakravarthi, Maharaja, Narendra, Parshnika, Pattadhara, Mandalesha, Pattabhaj, Praharaka and Ashtagraha*. Each class of palace is further classified into three types based on the measurements and the number of walls, levels, quarters, ditches, gardens etc. They are *jyeshta* or superior, *madhya* or intermediate and *kanishtha* or inferior.

N

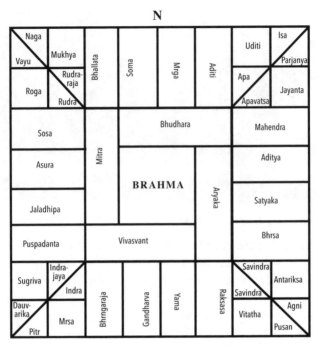

Manduka mandala

Fig. 09.01

The Sthapati or the master architect surveyed the site, tested the suitability of the soil and then selected the site for the township. While designing the *Rajanivesha* on the *Paramasayika mandala* or 81 module plan, the *Sthapati* designed a bordering moat (a deep, wide ditch surrounding a castle, fort, or town, filled with water and intended as a defence against attack) and a fortification for the palace. The reinforcement also incorporated surrounding walls that were laid out to make the whole palace look beautiful and well secured. The doors and gates were placed in exalted areas. The two doors of the palace are identified as *Vastudwara and Bhavanadwara*. *Vastudwara* was generally placed on the North of the structure and the *Bhavanadwara* on the east. The main gate (*Gopuradwara*) for the palace was placed in the North in the *Bhallata* module of the *Paramasayika* mandala. This identifies with the fourth (out of nine) module from the west. A door was placed on each cardinal direction—*Mahendra* on the East, *Pushpadanta* on the West, *Rakshasa* (*Grhakshatha*) on the south and *Bhallata* on the north. A gateway with a *gopuram*, which added to the opulence of the palace, was provided in each of the four directions. The palace also had secondary (or side) doors called *Pakshadwara* that were used when the main gates were closed. The *Brahma Peeta* or the royal temple was installed in the *Brahmastana* or the central part of the town.

Types of Fortification

The strengthening of the townships by fortification was an integral part of town planning. **Samarangana Sutradhara** speaks about two types of fortification natural and artificial. Natural fortifications are six fold water fort, mud fort, forest fort, desert fort, mountain fort and cave fort. These are inaccessible to hostile encroachments by their advantageous situation secured by natural defenses. Artificial strength refers to creating the parapets (elevations), ramparts(barricades) and moats (deep ditches.)

The layout of the area has the walls (*prakara*) running round the town parallel to the *ghantamarga* (pathways running round the boundaries of the town.) Width of these walls is mentioned in terms of hasta and varies on the nature of the township big, medium and small. Moats are dug at selected areas of the rampart and the trampling bulls pressed the earth dug out. The earth removed was made use of in leveling the other unleveled areas of the township. The cleaned and cleared moats were further strengthened with bricks and stones. They were then filled up with water drawn from the water reservoirs or tanks of the town.

Each moat was fitted with a mechanical device that periodically cleared the stagnant water. Well positioned lotus and lily plants were used to beautify the area. Well-bred crocodiles were placed in moats to prevent any enemy swimming to cross into the well-fortified fort. Orchards and flower gardens were laid in the inner area of the town. The external side of the town was planted with thorny plants. Kautilya's **Arthasastra** speaks of three Moats. The moats apart from being fortification to the town had also other usages; for instance, they also acted as drainage system of the town. The moats also supplied necessary mud for erecting the town walls (prakara) and for covering and levelling marshy lands of the town. They were also connected to the rivers so that in case of emergency, they could inundate the town.

The third step of fortification was the *prakara* or the parapet wall that was generally raised on the ramparts. The ramparts were made strong by filling them up with massive stones and were of specific widths and heights. The classical works recognize the minimum and maximum heights for the parapet walls that were built of bricks. Big stone slabs were also used but wood was not used. Mention is made of an intermediate passage

known as *deva patha*, which was meant for movement of chariots. The width of the bottom of the surrounding wall is also acknowledged. The ancient books generally identify a single *prakara* on the rampart. However, it is interesting to note that raising of towers referred to as *attalakas* that had moveable staircases for a comfortable ascent and descent. The fifth element of fortification was the gateways or gopurams of the town. These were pyramidal in shape. The gopurams are also known as *dwara attalaka*. Speaking of *dwaras* or doors, twelve principal gates on the pathways, *raja arga* (central streets) and *maharathya* in all the directions were used. Certain widths were also identified for each gate. Vastu treatises recognize four main gates, one each in the cardinal directions and calls them *brahma* (north), *aindra* (east), *yamya* (south) and *sainapatya* (West.) Minor gates were recommended.

Each gateway was provided with a smaller gateway which was known as *Pratoli*. They were provided with a flight of steps and a decorative small tower in which Weapons were housed. The pratoli was laid secure with broad and high doors that had door bolts.

Mohenjo Daro and Harappa

Looking back on Indian history, Mohenjo Daro and Harappa are the most ancient testimonies of extremely well planned cities. These ancient cities of India were laid out on a Vastu-based module formed by rectangular settlements and well laid out streets. The colonies consisted of a wide range of houses — small and big — some with a single courtyard and some with several courtyards. The sanitary systems were well laid out for both public and private use. The refined and elegant buildings speak of the application of the great science of Vastu to not only Harappa and Mohenjo Daro cities but also to a number of other well laid out ancient cities across the width and breadth of India. Architecture and civic life facilities were based on well-planned layouts, which mirror human dealings within a rational blueprint of the universe, where the laws of nature governed the building of cities and habitations. The magnificent ancient city of Jaipur is one of the other great Vastu based cities.

The ancient treatises on dwellings deal with city planning and building plans. Certain standards are set for the basic planning of towns and cities — site analysis, measurements, models of towns, location of temples and royal buildings, forts and fortification, placement of markets, roads and streets, etc. These standards also covered environmental and other concerns like lifestyles and activities. All these were based on one of the thirty-two plans that were referred to as *Vastu Purusha Mandala*.

We can identify many great forts of India. The Raigarh fort was occupied by Shivaji in 1656 and where he was crowned as Chatrapati Shivaji in 1674. This fort is a very well planned fort having pathways through secured strong holds and well placed observational towers. Other examples of well-planned forts are Panhala, Shivneri (near Bombay) and Jhanjira (in the midst of Arabian Sea) which is said to be constructed by Northeastern Africans. Jhanjira is identified with 19 citadels meant for maximum security with canons positioned such that the enemies could not locate the firing citadel. Daulatabad (originally said to be Devagiri) near Aurangabad is surrounded by moats on all the sides. Bundi, earlier known as Brindavati and Tara Garh is said to be built in1342 A.D. and has a height of 1400 feet. The ceilings and walls have wonderful paintings. The Jaisalmer Fort has two outer walls with 99 bastions. The temples, idols and sculptures speak of the excellence of Indian craftsman and artisans. Near Jaipur there is another fort called Kumbhalgarh with sturdy wall and ramparts all around and domes and arches that speak of strength, beauty and splendor of Indian architecture. The Rathambhor fort has reservoirs and streams designed for protection and is said to have masonry pipelines throughout. A beautiful temple of Lord Ganesha, which is also a marvel of architecture, built in the 8th century adorns the fort. The Golconda fort near Hyderabad is another exquisite marvel. The forts of Kalinjar, Red Fort, Chittorgarh, Gwalior, Bidar, Bijapur, Srirangapatnam, Vijayanagar, Chitradurga, Bekal, Trichy, Kanyakumari, Gingee, Chidambaram, Chandragiri, Anchuthengu (Kerala) and many other forts all over India are examples of splendid workmanship of the Sthapatis of India.

Summing up, fortification generally included exhaustive quantities of water, food, grains, medicines, weapons, big high and thick ramparts guarded on all sides, gates with stairways, some visible and others secret with double shutter doors and bars. Ramparts were square, circular or rectangular. A proper security meant the township was inaccessible and impregnable against attack by enemies and a haven for the residents of the township. The ancient masters have gifted us with a wealth of knowledge and we just need to apply their wisdom to our modern habitations such as houses, apartments, governmental buildings, corporate and business buildings, layouts, town planning etc. The skill needed is in adapting the traditional knowledge to the convenience and requirements of modem conditions. Vastu is an eternal knowledge available to help us to make our lives happier—spiritually and materially.

10

Cosmo-Terrestrial Energies

Vastu is slowly becoming an integral part of modern architecture. The ancient masters of this dwelling science arrived at certain basic thumb rules that defined the comfort, contentment and happiness of the residents of these Vastu-based structures. The wise men understood the cosmic energies coming from the millions of universes around us and their interaction with terrestrial energies when they referred to the Almighty as *Akhilanda Koti Brahmanda Nayaka* or the Lord of million Universes. In this chapter, let us try to understand the various energies and how our ancients defined the Vastu rules relative to them.

Cosmic energies or cosmic rays originate in outer space. They are said to travel at nearly the speed of light and impinge on the earth from all directions. These cosmic rays are said to be the nuclei of atoms, ranging from the lightest to the heaviest elements in the Periodic Table. Cosmic rays also include high energy electrons, positrons and other sub-atomic particles. The atmosphere slows down and is broken up.

Scientists have indicated that the cosmic rays are electrically charged and are influenced by the earth's magnetic field and they move in all directions.

Scientists have also indicated that thousands of cosmic rays pass through our bodies and our habitations every minute and the resulting radiation levels are relatively low corresponding to only a few percent of the natural background radiation at sea level.

Perhaps, when they identified certain rooms for certain activities on the Eastern grid, they thought of solar energies and their interaction with cosmic energies. The mandala or building plan recommended for *manushyalaya* or dwelling for a human is the *Paramasayika* mandala. Each side of the quadrangle of the site or construction is divided into 9 parts. This results in a total of 81 parts for the entire quadrangle. The solar radiation is split into 7+2 colours and the Eastern grid of the site or construction receives the colour spectrum.

Earth's Atmosphere

Let us now try to understand something about our atmosphere. The atmosphere, which is a blanket of air, surrounds the earth to the extent of almost 350 miles from its surface. We know that earth life is supported by the atmosphere along with the energies coming from the Sun in addition to the earth's magnetic fields. The atmosphere also filters the high energy cosmic energies.

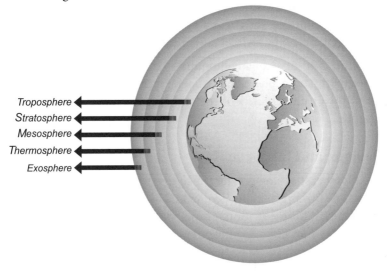

The envelope of gas surrounding the earth charges from the ground upwards. Four distinct layers - troposphere, stratosphere, mesosphere and thermosphere - have been identified using thermal characteristics (temperature changes), chemical composition, movement and density. The troposphere, that is stated to be the most dense of the layers, is the lowest region of the atmosphere, extending from the earth's surface to a height of about 6 miles. The tropopause is the boundary layer between the stratosphere and the troposphere. The first layer consisting of tropopause and troposphere is called the lower atmosphere.

The stratosphere extends to about 30 miles high. This part of the atmosphere is rather dry and less dense. Ultraviolet radiation begins to get absorbed. The ozone layer, which absorbs and scatters the solar ultraviolet radiation, is in this layer. The stratopause separates the stratosphere from the next layer which is mesosphere. This layer starts just the stratosphere and extends up to about 53 miles above the ground. The mesopause separates the stratosphere from the next layer. Stratosphere and mesosphere, along with stratopause and mesopause, are called the middle atmosphere by scientists.

The thermosphere starts just above the mesosphere and extends to about 350 miles from ground. The temperatures here increase with the increase in altitude due to the Sun's energy. This layer is known as the upper atmosphere. In the stratosphere, the region of the earth's atmosphere from above the surface, the chemical compound ozone plays a vital role in absorbing harmful ultraviolet and infrared radiation from the Sun.

It is seen that the ozone compound in the atmosphere (comprising of troposphere, stratosphere, mesosphere, thermosphere and exosphere) tempers the far end colours of the spectrum to make them naturally therapeutic.

Ultraviolet and Infra-red Rays

The Northeast sector is referred to as *Deva moola* or a spiritually elevated zone and is generally recommended for elderly and sick people, pregnant ladies, for meditation, prayer, study area for children etc. The colour spectrum of this zone includes the ultraviolet, violet and indigo colours. Ultraviolet light is said to be a disinfectant. Contaminated objects like surgical instruments, bedspreads, the air in a patient's room, human skin and blood, are said to be rapidly cleansed of viruses and bacteria.

Apart from the destroying of infectious organisms, it is said that ultraviolet light also stimulates the immune system. Today, Ultraviolet therapy is said to be effective in the following environments.

Bacterial - Infections of wounds, typhoid etc and viral infections - pneumonia, hepatitis, mumps, encephalitis, herpes, measles etc.

Chronic diseases like bronchial asthma, allergic conjunctivitis, hepatitis, kidney disease, eczema, migraine etc.

Inflammatory diseases like acne, allergic gastritis, arthritis, thyroiditis, boils, sinusitis etc.

Other ailments like tumor, exhaustion disease due to improper circulation, varicose and diabetic ulcer, some types of gangrene and vascular headache, non-healing wounds and delayed union of fractures.

The ancient masters, based on their scientific acumen and intuition, possibly felt that the Northeast sector was a very important area for health and identified it as *Deva Moola, Eashanya* or Space of God.

Around 1800, William Herschel observed that the temperatures of colours increased from the violet to the red part of the spectrum. The portion of the spectrum beyond the red part not visible to the naked eye is named infra-red and apparently is devoid of sunlight. However, this region has the highest temperature of all. Vastu identifies this area as Agneya or Southeast.

Infrared has therapeutic value of heating the body for better health, healing and greater vitality. Infra-red therapy is said to relieve chronic pain, arthritis, back pain etc. It also improves the circulation by stimulating blood flow and consequently increases energy levels and promotes healing capabilities and overall health. In fact, this therapy is also said to help to burn calories! Vastu experts recommend a cooking area or a kitchen in the Southeast sector of an area that covers three colours of the spectrum— orange, red and infra-red.

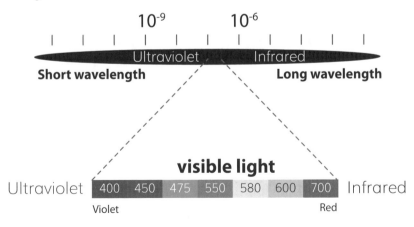

In concluding, let us remember that my revered father Dr. B. V. Raman often mentioned that our ancient masters were not hair-splitting philosophers but men of great scientific knowledge and wisdom. They also possessed the extraordinary tool of intuition, and with its help, they arrived at certain primary or fundamental laws of Vastu. They understood the vital importance of the cosmic energies and their interaction with terrestrial energies. Vastu aims at creating health, happiness and contentment to mankind by appropriate location, orientation and construction of buildings.

11

Natural Calamities

THE natural calamities (earthquakes, tsunamis and cyclones) in Pakistan, Indonesia, the coastal belts of Sri Lanka and India and earlier in Gujarat and in Orissa left thousands (perhaps lakhs) dead and homeless. Many were injured, many maimed and countless orphaned. Many of these people are still trying to put their lives and properties together and stand on their legs.

On January 26th 2001, an earthquake measuring 6.9 on the Richter scale hit Gujarat. With the epicenter about 20 kilometers Northeast of Bhuj, Anjar and Bachau in Kutch and Gandhi dham in the vicinity of Kandla were also equally devastated. Ahmedabad too had its share when huge buildings collapsed within minutes of the tremors.

The Rann of Kutch, in fact, had been marked as an extremely high-risk earthquake zone. Had our engineers taken a cue of this fact, perhaps there could have been lesser deaths and lesser destruction of properties. Citing the Gujarat earthquake, an architecture professor of the University of Washington says that earthquakes have proven deadly because building contractors skimp on materials.

There were quakes in El Salvador in Central America and in Seattle, U.S.A. Seattle escaped with relatively little damage after a 6.8 magnitude earthquake, one of the worst in 50 years, hit it, presumably for two reasons:

- The depth of the quake center (the quake's epicenter was 48 km below ground.)

- Good construction. (Most buildings constructed in Seattle over the past 25 years or so were built to a uniform code designed to withstand strong earthquakes.)

The powerful quake that ripped through the region on Wednesday, the 28th February 2001 caused few serious injuries and only a fraction of the property damage that the similar sized tremors did to the Gujarat cities.

Ancient Masters

Were our ancient masters who laid down the laws of Vastu aware of the destructive powers of natural calamities? Did they think of these phenomena when they wrote their texts? They did think of earthquakes, cyclones and other natural phenomena when they gave us information about ways and means of construction. They spoke of soil evaluation before construction began. Soil suitability and strength received prime importance.

Our ancients believed that a foundation of a building was much more than combination of bricks, mortar, concrete, steel etc. They felt that laying a foundation was a symbolic homage to Mother Earth by man and every possible care to strengthen it was necessary.

They particularly talked about depth of a foundation (*Bhumilamba.*) In fact ancient treatises on Vastu Sastra have customarily advised a foundation that is equal to a man's stature plus his length of hand. Today's engineers tell us that six to seven feet of foundation is necessary for a normal height building to be firm and secure. Our masters also highlighted the importance of the base (*Adhishtana*) being as high as the foundation.

They spoke of the importance of pillars and colums in making a building strong. They talked about decreasing heights for each floor of the building. We notice that ancients built multi-storeyed buildings such that the height of each floor slowly reduced as they went up. In fact **Brihat Samhita** of Varahamihira tells us the each floor should be less than the floor below it by 1/12th its height. *They may have deduced that during an earthquake or other natural calamities such a building could sway but not fall.*

Earthquakes themselves do not kill people, but badly constructed buildings do. Being aware of this fact our ancients gave importance to every aspect of foundation including the materials used. They spoke of the need to vibe with *Nature* by using construction materials like bricks (*Ishtika*), stone (*Shila*) and wood (*Kaashta* or *Gahana*.) The ancient classical texts also spoke of wood as basic material not only for doors, windows, and cabinets but also for structures too.

In fact, it is commonly known in engineering that wood absorbs shock evenly and a house built out of wood is unlikely to collapse. Wood and steel are said to be ductile and less prone to seismic disturbances.

Importance of *Paisacha*

Our ancients while speaking of buildings have highlighted *Paischa* zone of a *Mandala*. They divide an area into four concentric zones. The inner zone is *Brahma*, the next is *Daiva*, and the third zone is *Manushya* and the fourth zone is *Paisacha*. They have very clearly specified construction on the <u>*Daiva*</u> and *Manushya* zones and totally disapproved of construction on the *Paisacha* zone.

To apply this to present times, we need to construct the building away from the compound so that it does not touch the neighbor's wall. Modern Engineering Science tells us that adjacent buildings should be separated by sufficient distance to prevent hammering each other in case of seismic disturbances!

Another – important uncompromising thumb rule of our masters of wisdom was in respect of the shape of a structure. Our ancient writers have invariably recommended square, rectangular, circular and other regular shapes. Irregular shapes have been prohibited.

The square (*Chaturasra*) is the fundamental, essential and perfect form of Indian Architecture. A square presupposes the circle and in fact results from it. Expanding energy shapes the circle from the center and then establishes itself in the shape of a square. In a square, the primary elements of Nature (*Pancha Mahabhootas*) are also said to be in perfect balance The *Chaturasra*, because of its perfect shape is considered sacred and superior in Indian Architecture. We find today's engineering principles telling us that geometric shapes like squares, rectangles and circles disperse seismic forces equally in all directions and are therefore safe in the case of natural calamities. Irregular shapes result in uneven distribution of forces thereby making buildings prone to collapse!

The cyclones of Orissa and the earthquakes of Gujarat saw most modern buildings collapse. Yet these devastating forces of nature could not disturb many temples built hundreds of years ago based on certain principles of the ancients masters rooted in Vedic tradition. Are these not proof of the great scholarship of our ancient masters of architecture? Are these not proof of the fact that they were aware of many of the known and unknown laws of Nature and their relationship to man and his buildings?

It is the right time for us modern people to study the various treatises of ancient Indian architecture. Our architects and engineers have just to take what our Vedic seers have handed over to us on a platter and apply it to the modern buildings so that the residents live in security, safety and happiness.

The 2004 Indian Ocean earthquake and tsunami occurred at 07:58:53 in local time on 26 December, with an epicentre off the west coast of northern Sumatra, Indonesia. It was an undersea megathrust earthquake that registered a magnitude of 9.1–9.3 Mw, reaching a Mercalli intensity up to IX in certain areas.

Generally Vastu refers to the energies from the Northwest and Southeast as disturbing energies. It is pertinent to note here that the earlier earth quakes of Gujarat and Seattle took place in the northwest of India and America respectively. The earthquake in Indonesia at the far end of the year 2004 that devastated crores worth of property and killed more than 1,50,000 people spread across 12 nations.

On December 26, 2004, an earthquake with an estimated magnitude of 9.1 struck the coast of Sumatra, Indonesia. Reports say that 2,27,898 people were killed or listed as missing and presumed dead. Material losses in the Indian Ocean region were $10 billion.

The tidal waves generated by the earthquake travelled southeast to the coastal belt of Tamilnadu, Orissa, Sri Lanka, Andaman and Nicobar and other places and killed thousands of innocent people .

A careful observation reveals that the tsunami tidal waves moved along the Northwest - Southeast diagonal to hit India & Sri Lanka. It is unfortunate that destruction of property and people of this magnitude has taken place. In India, the entire coastal belt of Tamilnadu consisting of Chennai, Nagapittinam, Cuddalore has suffered major losses. The powerful earthquake on the 8th October 2005 that rocked parts of Pakistan and killed over forty thousand people in Pakistan and India and caused immense loss of property and kind. United Nations officials have estimated that one million people were homeless, hungry and threatened by disease. This earthquake too occurred to the Northwest of India.

11

In a Nutshell

Given Below are vital and important aspects of Vastu.

For residences and business houses, use the *Paramasayika Mandala* (plan) and for temples, use the *Manduka* (Page 66) or *Asana Mandala*.

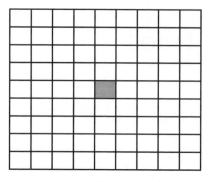

Paramasayika Mandala

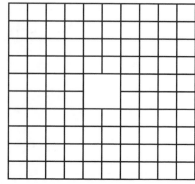

Asana Mandala

- Have the compound (perimeter) walls on all the four sides.
- Have the building away from the compound walls. Allow more space on the East and North.
- Have the well, bore-well and/or under ground water tank in the North of Northeast.
- Have your building built at least three feet above the road level.
- *Paschima Sala* and *Dakshina Sala* buildings (facing East and North) are good.
- Have the main entrance in the exalted zones depending on the road.
- Have a corresponding exit door on the other side of the building.
- Let the building (and furniture) be oriented towards the four cardinal directions only (East, South, West and North.)
- Let the main and the exit doors be the biggest and the smallest doors respectively.
- Two-shutter doors are the best.
- Keep the centre of the building and the centre of the site free from any loads, beams, pillars, columns, depressions, wells etc.
- Keep the north and east open by having your verandah in these directions.

- Avoid having the *Griha Nabhi* (centre of the structure) to the *Ageneya* (Southeast) or *Vayuvya* (Northwest) of the *Brahma Nabhi* (centre of the site.)

- Grow *Tulsi* (Basil), *Tumbe* (Common Leucas) and other herbal plants in the North and East. The former two plants are sacred to Lord Vishnu and Siva respectively

- Place the cupboards containing important documents, currency, jewels etc. in the corner of the Northwest portion of the master room in a locker that opens up to the top.

- The master's (the responsible person of the home or office) place is *Nirutya* or Southwest. Sleep in the southwest sector of the room with the head to the south. Let not the cots touch the walls.

- The Southeast can be for the kitchen. Face the East while cooking. Let the sink be towards the North or East of Northeast of the kitchen.

- The Car Garage can be in the Southeast or Northwest sector.

- South, Southeast and East rooms are ideal for men and boys and North, Northwest and West rooms for women and girls.

- The Northwest can be for Guest Rooms, Garages, Toilets, Guest Rooms and Granaries.

- The Pooja (or meditation) room can be in the center of the building or in the Northeast sector.

- The medicine chests can also be in the northeast or east sector for enhancing the healing properties of the medicines.

- Grow deep rooted trees in the west and south, in that order. Coconut, ashoka, guava, neem are all good. Avoid banyan trees at homes.

- Have as many windows as needed in all the directions. Only take care that the total surface area of the openings on the north and east is more than the surface area on the south and west.

- Staircases can be in west, south, southwest, northwest and southeast sides. See that the final step upwards is either towards south or west.

- Have the mirrors only on east or north walls. When you have your sinks on the north or east wall, the mirrors automatically come right.

- Let the overhead tank be on the west of southwest without touching the Southwest – Northeast diagonal.

- If higher elevations are neded, let the south and west of the building be higher.

- Have the cellars/basements in the north, east or northeast portion of your building.

- Have a Swastika or Om (preferably etched on copper) installed on the *Mahadwara* (main door.)

- Elders and ill-people can sleep with their heads to the south and youngsters (students) with their heads to the east.

- Improve the digestion by sitting on a wooden chair or wooden platform and by avoiding body contact with others while eating.

- Don't sleep or sit under beams.

- Heavy furniture can be placed in the south or west and light furniture in the north or east.

- Draw electrical energy into your house from the southeast of your house.

- Never have your furnace room in the southwest or northeast of your home.

- Never sleep on the room above your furnace room.

- Have the exhaust fans in the northwest/southeast sector of your rooms.

- Photos of departed souls can adorn the south walls. Photos of living persons and deities can be in the east and north walls.

- Pregnant ladies can avoid proximity to televisions, computers and other electric and electronic equipment. Avoid smart phones in their pockets.

- They can avoid sleeping with their heads to the west and north.

- Avoid depressions and water areas in the centre of your site/building.

- For human habitation, avoid *madhya dwara* (middle doors.)

The information presented above is for the purpose of providing merely an overview of Vastu. It is to be remembered that the application of Vastu to an existing structure or a proposed construction needs to be carefully done. The various intricate elements of Nature have to be balanced to ensure that the owner or resident of the dwelling is benefited from the application of Vastu.